S H A R Y N C R A I G

Layer 'em Up #2

Volume 2: Basically Boxes

Table of Contents

D1133722

Layer 'em Up #2

Author: Sharyn Squier Craig
Publisher: Daniela Stout
Project Editor: Amy Falco
Graphics Editor: Amy Falco
Production Coordinator: Andie Stevenson
Operations Coordinator: Diane Lee

First Printing

ISBN: 978-0-9795316-8-2

ISBN: 978-0-9795316-8-2

5 2 3 9 5

9 780979 531682

sharyncraig@cox.net

Acknowledgments

I would never be able to write the books I write without assistance from a lot of people. I would like to take a few minutes now to thank those that made this book possible.

My husband has always been my biggest fan and strongest supporter. Thank you, George, for understanding how important quilting is to me, and for realizing that it's equally important that I share my passion with other quilters.

My daughter, Amy, designed this book, created the illustrations, and made sure the words made sense. Without her amazing talent, you would not be reading this book today. Amy, I really appreciate all your time and talents. Thank you for working with me on this project.

I must thank my Oncall Quilters: Sandy Andersen, Pat Hook, Laurine Leeke, Margret Reap, Marnie Santos, and Carolyn Smith, for testing the technique and making quilts, many that appear in this book, and some that don't. Every time I ask for help they never question, complain, or say no. Instead they ask only, "How soon do you need it?" Before I know it, they appear with quilts and constructive comments. Thank you, ladies! I definitely couldn't do this without you.

Thank you Judi Sample, Robin Ruiz, and Liz Henselmeier for machine quilting the tops in record time. Your incredible stitching enhanced the quilts and made them come alive. I appreciate your talents and timeliness.

I need to thank Moda Fabrics for providing many of the Layer Cakes™ that I've used throughout the quilts. Those pre-cut 10" squares are wonderful building blocks. The inspiration of having them right here, ready to go, was a huge help. And a big thanks to Moda Fabrics and Robert Kaufman Fabrics for supplying the fabric we used in the step-by-step illustrations.

And another big thank you to Maureen Cuddington and Carolyn Ketterer for testing the written instructions and making sure everything was written correctly.

Last, but by no means least, is Daniela Stout. Daniela owns Cozy Quilt Shop and Cozy Quilt Designs™ publishing company. Little did I know when her shop opened several years ago how special she would become to me. Daniela, your friendship and support has been amazing. Thank you for taking a chance on these books. Thank you for encouraging me throughout the process, and thank you for your friendship.

~ Sharyn

Introduction

Sharyn Craig

Over 20 years ago I made my first quilt using this layering concept. At the time, I didn't think too much about it. I just saw it as an easy, efficient, and organized way to build quilts. Being efficient and organized has always been of utmost importance to me when making quilts. I don't like chaos, and I hate to rip. If I'm not organized, I can quickly find myself in the midst of chaos and making mistakes which, of course, leads to having to rip. My motto has always been: "There has to be an easier way."

In 2003, I got serious about turning this layering technique into something more than the occasional quilt. I started making more and more quilts using the system. Each quilt I made enabled me to fine tune the concept just a little bit more. The first of the Layer 'em Up books came out spring of 2009. In that book, I focused on blocks that slice squares diagonally to create Xs and other related blocks. Now we're turning our attention to square-inspired designs or "boxes."

Each of the four patterns found in this book start with squares of fabric that get layered one on top of another, then sliced in different ways. Next comes the scrambling, which means you mix up the pieces to create different colorations for the square-in-a-square look. I'll give you directions for both the order to scramble the pieces, as well as how you will sew the pieces back together. There will be no guesswork on your part.

Most importantly, this book includes a lot of inspiring quilts. There are no patterns and no specific recipes for making a particular quilt. You will have instructions for the block process. You will have cutting measurement guidelines. You will know how to make the quilts any size you wish with any number of fabrics. It's up to you to take this information and create your own masterpieces.

This system is good for beginner and experienced quilters alike. The blocks are incredibly fast, very fun, and extremely forgiving. These quilts are so much fun, and so fast, that they are perfect for community service quilts, baby quilts, off-to-college quilts, etc. But don't be fooled into thinking that they are only good for quilts you are giving away. With a bit of focused thinking and fabric selection, you can make quilts that feel like art quilts. You can make quilts that you'll be proud to hang on your walls. There is no end to the direction these quilts can take. So, now, let's not waste any more time. Let's get quilting!

Basic Supplies

- **Sewing Machine** — Be sure to clean and oil your machine and replace the needle before beginning any new project.

- **Rotary Cutter** — You'll be cutting through lots of layers with these projects, so make sure your rotary cutter has a new, sharp blade. With each new project, a new blade is in order.

TLC for your rotary cutter:
Periodically you should take it apart and clean out all the lint that collects between the blade and the plastic shield. Once you clean out the lint, it is advised that you replace the oil that was there when you bought the cutter. The oil that you need is nothing more than sewing machine oil. One drop of oil before you put the blade back on the cutter will prolong the life of your blade dramatically.

Another thing that will make your cutter perform better is NOT to overtighten the screw when putting it back together. Here's a simple test you can perform: open your cutter and hold it lightly between your thumb and index finger. See if the blade turns freely and easily with no pressure or pushing. If you have to push the cutter to turn the blade, and there's no fabric involved, then imagine how hard you'll have to push when you have four or six or eight layers of fabric! If you have to use force to turn the blade, loosen the screw.

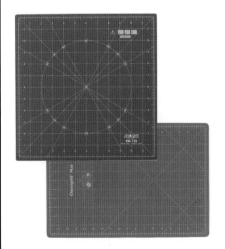

- **Mat** — When making these quilts, I really like the rotating mat by Olfa®. They come in different sizes, but the 12" square will work for all the blocks we make in this book. If you don't have an Olfa® rotating mat, then a small scale mat such as 12" x 18" will work.

- **Acrylic Rulers — Square Rulers and Strip Cutting Rulers**
Square Rulers: You'll definitely want to have a 10" square – such as the one by Cozy Quilt Designs™. You may also find it helpful to have other square rulers on hand, depending on the size block you choose to make, but you can square and true up your blocks to smaller sizes using the 10".

Strip Rulers: I suggest the 6" x 12", 2" x 18", or 4" x 14".

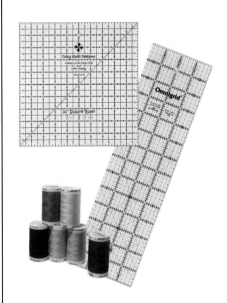

- **Thread** – I recommend high quality, 50 weight, 100% cotton thread.

Selecting Fabrics

Depending on the type and colors of fabrics you choose, you can have anything from a whimsical quilt for a child to a sophisticated piece of wall art. It's all about the fabric.

If you find yourself overwhelmed with fabric selection, it might help to have a goal in mind— a grandchild, a child going off to college, your aunt in a nursing home, your husband's office wall. Whatever the goal, whoever the lucky recipient, if you know what you're ultimately going to do with the quilt, selecting colors can be easier. For a baby you might pick pastels or bright colors. For a son going off to college, you can select his school colors. If your aunt's favorite color is purple, well, that solution is obvious! Selecting colors with a person in mind can definitely jump-start the process.

"STARTER" FABRICS

If you're drawn to a multi-colored piece of fabric, use that as inspiration when selecting your quilt colors. It doesn't have to end up in the quilt — or maybe you'll use it as the backing — but it's a great starting point.

Another way I often begin the fabric selection process is to pick a single piece of fabric that I really like. I call this the "starter" fabric. This fabric is a multi-colored print that I can draw colors from for my quilt. I know that if I like the colors in that "starter" piece, I'm probably going to like the finished quilt. Once I have that first piece I look for other fabrics to go with it. I choose a variety of print scales . . . large florals, small calicos, plaids, tonals, stripes. You don't want all your fabrics to be busy, multi-colored fabrics, unless you want a busy, high-energy quilt.

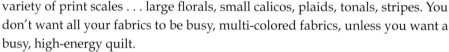

Another option you might want to employ in picking fabrics is to think of three colors that you like together. That's how I started Band Box 1 (shown on the next page). I love blues, greens, and browns together. Before I pulled the first piece of fabric, I made the deliberate decision to use more brown and blue fabrics with green as the accent color. I pulled from my stash and made a pile of fabric on my cutting table, just mixing them randomly. After you make your pile, stand back and view what you've created. If it feels good, then you're ready to start cutting squares. Remember, you don't have to limit yourself to these fabrics, nor do you have to use everything you've selected. I'd rather have too many fabrics and eliminate some if they end up not working. At the same time as I'm making the blocks, if I suddenly want more colors or fabrics, I add them. That's how I ended up adding the rust and gold tones. It didn't take a lot of those add-on colors to punch up the quilt, but I feel better with the final result!

NOTE

One of the great things about this technique is that you need one starting square for every one finished block you want to make. Look at pages 30 - 31 to determine how many blocks (and how many starting squares) you need for the size quilt you want to make.

Another thing to keep in mind is that you want prints of different scale. It's easy to fall into the trap of always using the same type of fabrics: small scale florals, tonals, plaids, large prints, etc. But, you need a little bit of everything. Use more of what you're most comfortable with, but tweak it with bits of other scale or type fabrics for the best results. Don't be afraid to throw in a few batiks or reproduction-type fabrics to add an interesting spark.

It's important to know that all of the quilts we're going to make start with squares. For most of the starting square sizes, you can use pre-cut 10" squares that many quilt shops are selling, such as the Moda Layer Cakes™. I don't use all the fabrics in any one collection or grouping. I don't stick to just one line of fabric. If I like fabrics together, I use them together. If I don't like them together, I don't put them together. But these bundles get me started.

I also like to add fabrics from my "stash." One reason I do this is to justify all those fabrics that I have. But more importantly, I do it because it makes the quilts more interesting. I've been building my stash for over 30 years. For me, mingling the different fabrics together adds a depth to the finished quilt that is missing when I don't do this. I love buying fabric. But I often find the best quilts come from using some new and some old fabrics at the same time.

All of the quilts you will see in this book have three things in common. They are fast, fun, and very forgiving. When you make blocks quickly, it is less traumatic if one or two don't live up to your expectations. The bottom line here is that I want you to have fun making these quilts, so relax and enjoy the process.

Fabric: To Pre-Wash or Not To Pre-Wash

Honestly, there is no right or wrong answer here. I have been making quilts for more than 30 years, and I have ALWAYS washed my fabric the minute it gets into the house; before it ever enters my sewing room. Having said that, there really is no good way to wash the 10" pre-cut square packages and the strip bundles, etc., that are on the market today, so I don't. To answer your next question, yes, I do mix my stash (washed fabric) with the unwashed 10" squares I buy.

I hear what you're thinking now, "But what's going to happen to my quilt when I wash it?" I am not going to be responsible for your quilts, but my personal experience has been that as long as there is plenty of quilting to hold the layers together, nothing adverse is going to happen. If you're worried about color bleeding, and who isn't, then you might put a Shout Color Catcher™ (available at many quilt shops and in your grocery store laundry aisle) in the washing machine when you wash the quilt. If there's any color loss, it will transfer to these Color Catcher™ sheets, and not to other areas of your quilt.

Band Box 1

This quilt has 35 blocks set straight. With the Layer 'em Up method you have to make even numbers of blocks, so I had to make 36 blocks in order to have 35 for the quilt. I never worry about extra blocks. I save all my extras knowing that someday they'll work in another quilt. You might even use that extra block for a label on your quilt.

Basic Instructions For The System

Each quilt in this book is based on a system of layering, slicing, scrambling, sewing, ironing, and squaring up. The descriptions that follow will help clarify each of these terms.

LAYER

Begin by positioning the suggested number of fabrics right sides up, one on top of another, matching the edges of the squares as closely as you can. It's not necessary to be perfect, just close. Follow the instructions in each section for the number of fabrics and the color or value arrangement needed. Remember, each fabric square represents one block in your quilt.

(Six layers in this stack.)

SLICE

Next you will slice through the layers as described in each specific pattern.* A sharp rotary cutter blade will make this part of the process easier. You will be given recommended Measurements For Slicing (MFS). Feel free to use these measurements as guidelines only. You may feel one of the numbers is too small and another too big, so change them! Most of the patterns can be cut randomly, rather than using all the same MFS. If you look closely at the quilts in this book, you will see that far more of them have been cut with random measurements rather than using the same for all the blocks.

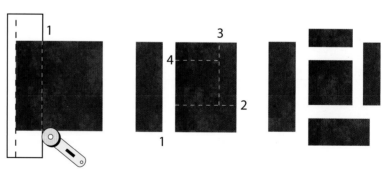

A small mat that can be rotated will make slicing your blocks that much easier. The Olfa® rotating mat described in the Basic Supplies is my personal favorite, but any small mat that can be easily turned will work. If you are not using a rotating mat, when it comes time to rotate things, you will need to pick up your mat and rotate it. Do not attempt to lift your fabric once you've begun slicing.

Make sure that as you slice each piece, you slide it apart from the rest of the square before making the next cut. You don't want to cut through the previous section accidentally.

*NOTE

If you have a series of MFS numbers, cut them in the order they are listed. For example: 3", 3", 2", 2", would mean you make the first and second cuts at 3" and the third and fourth cuts at 2".

TIP

Make sure that as you slice each piece, you slide it apart from the rest of the square before making the next cut. You don't want to cut through the previous section accidentally!

8

SCRAMBLE

Once you slice the fabrics, you need to mix them up (scramble) before sewing them together. You'll find a unique scrambling diagram in every chapter, with numbers indicating how many pieces to take from the top of each pile and move to the bottom of that same pile.

Example: If there is a zero (0), you leave it alone. If there is a one (1), you take one fabric piece from the top and move it to the bottom. A two (2) means move two pieces to the bottom, and so on.

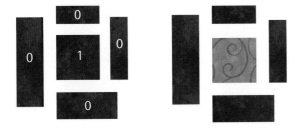

SEW

Follow the numbered illustrations provided in the individual chapters to sew the blocks together. The numbers positioned between the pieces indicate which pieces you sew together, and in what order.

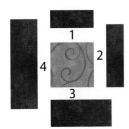

I recommend chaining the first seam of each block in your stack before starting seam #2. This means that you will sew seam #1 for each block unit in that particular set, one after another. Then you will sew seam #2 for each block, chaining them one after the other. Repeat with seam #3, then seam #4. In order to make sure you keep the pieces in the original order, follow these steps:

1. After all #1 seams are sewn, remove the block units from the sewing machine. Beginning with the last block unit sewn, clip the units apart.

2. As you clip the units apart, position the block units one on top of another. When you finish clipping and stacking, the last unit sewn will be on the bottom and the first unit sewn will be on top.

HINT

In our illustrations, a solid fill color on a block piece represents the backside of a fabric.

3. Finger press the seam allowance (S.A.) from the first block unit as specified, then sew seam #2 as indicated by the numbering system on the block. Finger press the S.A. on the piece for the second block unit, then add the piece for seam #2 for that second block. Continue chaining the remaining block units in your stack this same way.

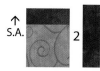

IRON

Once the blocks are all sewn together, you can iron them firmly. Whether you use steam or not is up to you. Personally, I always use steam for a nice flat block. You always want to iron the blocks BEFORE you square them up. Iron from the wrong side first so you can control what is happening with the seam allowances. Then turn the block over (right side up) and do the final firm ironing.

SQUARE UP

The easiest way to square up your blocks is by using a square ruler the size of your blocks. All you need to do is center the ruler on your block and trim all the way around. If you don't have the specific size ruler, then use the numbers on a square ruler that is larger than required.

A note about the square up size . . . your blocks may end up smaller or larger than what I indicate that they will be. That can happen if your seam allowance is not a scant quarter-inch. This can also happen if your thread is too thick. Not all 50 weight threads are created equal. The fatter your thread, the more space it occupies in the seam allowance, and the smaller your block might be. Just remember, you can make your blocks any size you need to, you just want them to all be the same size in the end for ease of sewing them together in your quilt.

Finishing Instructions

LAY OUT YOUR BLOCKS AS DESIRED

When you arrange your blocks, make sure you don't position blocks with the same fabrics too close together. With some fabrics the positioning won't matter, but with visually graphic, strong, or high energy fabrics, it will make a difference. If something bothers you, move it!

SEW THE TOP TOGETHER

Begin by sewing your blocks together into rows. I recommend alternating the seam allowances in row one all to the right, row two to the left, row three to the right, etc. Alternating the seam allowances this way allows them to butt up against one another and creates a better fit.

Then sew all the rows together.

Finally, iron your top carefully and thoroughly, being careful not to stretch or distort the edges. Check the top for flatness and remove any stray threads popping out of the seams.

BORDER

For these quilts, I suggest the following borders:

For 3" finished blocks:
- 1" cut size for the first border (Accent Border).
- 2½" cut size for the second border (Framing Border).

For 6", 7", and 8" finished blocks:
- 1½" cut size for the first border (Accent Border).
- 5½" cut size for the second border (Framing Border).

When attaching the borders, carefully pin at least every 5" to prevent the border strips from ruffling along the edges. I like to iron the border strip in place on the quilt, pin it, then sew it. Ironing first helps prevent the ruffling as well.

Iron border seam towards the next border strip you're adding each time.

It doesn't matter whether you add the side borders first, or the top and bottom borders, just be consistent.

Band Box — Quilts to Inspire...

Band Box 2

For this Band Box quilt, I followed my suggested Measurement for Slicing (MFS) and all the blocks here have identical cuts. This is the only Band Box sample that does. I selected the colors for this quilt (black, green, brown, and gold tones) after finding my "starter fabric," which ended up as the border. There are 24 blocks, therefore I needed to select 24 fabrics and cut squares. There isn't much high contrast, and there doesn't have to be, as long as you can see between each layer.

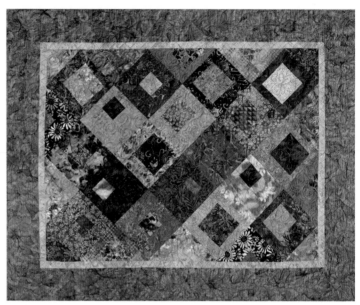

Batik 1

This quilt, and Batik 2 (on page 32), were made from the same set of blocks. I started with about 40 batik squares and made two different quilts. Batik 1 has 18 blocks set on point. For the side triangles I cut some of my extra blocks in half. In order for this to work size wise I had to trim my original 18 blocks down by one-half inch. By doing that, the extra blocks were exactly the right size for slicing corner to corner and making the side setting triangles. You do need to be careful if you decide to do this, because now you have the bias grain along the outside edges of your quilt. If you treat it carefully during ironing, you should be fine. Incidentally, I cut two different solid squares, which I sliced once corner to corner for the four corner triangles. You can find the sizes you need in the chart on page 31.

Band Box 3 (Also on the cover)

I used Moda's "Authentic" Layer Cake™ as the inspiration for the colors in this quilt, adding many additional fabrics from my stash. I created a total of 24 blocks for this quilt; 18 of them (squared to 7 ½") set on point, five (squared to 8") were sliced once, corner to corner, for the side setting triangles, and one (squared to 8 ½") was sliced twice for the corner triangles.

BAND BOX BLOCK

STARTING SQUARE	MEASUREMENT FOR SLICING*	SQUARING UP SIZE	FINISHED BLOCK SIZE
10"	3", 3", 2", 2"	8 ½"	8"
9"	3", 3", 2", 2"	7 ½"	7"
8"	2 ½", 2 ½", 2", 2"	6 ½"	6"
5"	1 ½", 1 ½", 1 ½", 1 ½"	3 ½"	3"

*The MFS is meant as a guideline only. I prefer more random numbers, meaning every group of layered fabrics I work with will have a different set of numbers.

Use the chart at the top of this page to select the finished block size you want to make. Then, use the charts on pages 30-31 to select the size quilt you want to make and see how many blocks you need to make for the size quilt you selected. Remember, if you want a quilt with 24 blocks, you'll begin with 24 squares of fabric, 48 blocks is 48 squares, etc.

NOTE: There is a difference of 2" from the starting square to the finished block size. If you want a different finished block size than I've provided, all you have to do is add 2" to your desired finished size to find the new starting square.

LAYER YOUR SQUARES

Select four, six, or eight starting squares of fabric. The fabrics can be high, medium, or low contrast. You can create the contrast through color only, or a combination of color and value. You just want to make sure you can see the difference between the various layers. You also want to make sure you like how the top fabric and the bottom fabric look next to each other.*

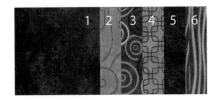

Stack all squares together, RIGHT SIDES UP, aligning the outer edges carefully.

(Six layers in this stack.)

NOTE: You can make these blocks with any EVEN number of fabrics in the stacks (2, 4, 6, or 8). You can work with as few as two if you prefer, but know if you do that, the two fabrics will just reverse position. The more fabrics in your stack, the greater variety you get in your blocks.

Box style quilts have been popular for some time now. To me, the center box in this block appears banded, hence its name. If you study the quilts included in this section, you'll see a variety of band widths, different positions for the inside square, and some inside squares that are not squares at all, but rectangles! This layering technique is an incredibly simple way to make all that happen in your blocks. If you want all your blocks identical, you need to use the same MFS every time. If you want your blocks to have greater variety, then relax and cut randomly!

*TIP

Check the first and last fabric squares and make sure the fabrics work well together as they will become part of the same block through the scrambling sequence.

SLICE

Using the illustration below as a guide, slice through the stack of squares. The chart at the beginning of this section gave you some possible measurements to use. Feel free to change them as desired.

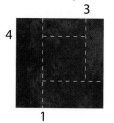

After each cut, you will move that section of pieces away from the remaining square, rotate your mat one quarter turn to the right and make the next cut. Repeat until you make all four cuts.

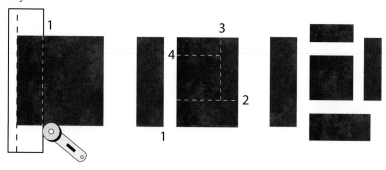

SCRAMBLE

There's only one piece to move on these blocks. So, as illustrated, take one piece from the top of the center section and move it to the bottom of the stack.

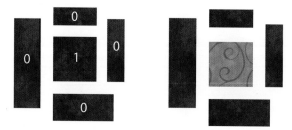

SEW

Follow the numbers for sewing. Take the first two pieces of the top block for seam #1, and sew them together. Continue with block two, then block three, etc., until seam #1 for all block units is sewn in this stack. As described on page 9 of the Basic Instructions, clip the units apart and stack one on top of another so the first unit is back on top.

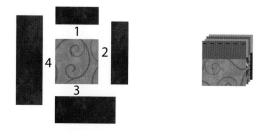

Finger press the seam allowance (S.A.) on the top unit, always away from the center square, and continue sewing with seam #2. Finger press the seam allowance (S.A.) on the second block unit and sew. Repeat with the remaining block units, sewing one after another.

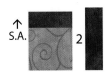

Follow the same procedure with seam #3 and then #4. When sewing the block, you'll be using one strip from the left each time, counter clockwise. We cut by moving to the right, and we sew by moving to the left.

NOTE: Don't panic at the unevenness of the outer edges. This is the way it is supposed to be at this point. We'll be fixing that later when we square up the blocks.

> **Depending on which piece is on top when you sew, your extensions may be at the opposite end than what we show in the illustrations. Both give you the same block in the end. You are still going to be trimming all extensions and squaring up all blocks.**

IRON

Once you've sewn all four seams of your blocks, you can go to the ironing board and iron them. Iron from the wrong side first to make sure all the seam allowances are going away from the inside square. Once you've lightly ironed from the wrong side, turn the block over, right side up, and do a firm ironing.

SQUARE UP

Refer to the chart on page 13 for the size to square up your blocks based on the size fabric square you started with. If you can't make your blocks the recommended size, don't worry, but do make sure all your blocks are the same size, whatever it is. Remember, space permitting, you can tilt the ruler on the block for a more off-kilter look. One way to definitely achieve this effect is to square your block up to a size smaller than originally suggested.

See page 11 for Finishing Instructions to complete your quilt top.

TIP

When sewing seams #2, #3, and #4, you'll find it helpful to keep the piece with the original square on TOP each time. That keeps the excess strip out of the way.

TIP

The pieces that you're adding to the original square should all be the same fabric. If you notice that it isn't the same fabric that means you've gotten them out of order. Refer to the Basic Instructions on pages 8 – 9 if you need a refresher on the basic piecing system.

Around the Box — Quilts to Inspire...

Pat's Oriental
by Pat Hook

Pat started with over 60 different oriental fabric squares to make the quilt showcased here. The blocks are set straight, 7 x 9, for this impressive quilt.

Margret's Boxes
by Margret Reap

Who said you can't put sashing with these blocks? When Margret first put her blocks on the wall she was not happy with how flat they appeared, so she started to play, looking for a way to perk them up. She selected black and red fabrics for sashing, combined them with that fun yellow, and that did the trick!

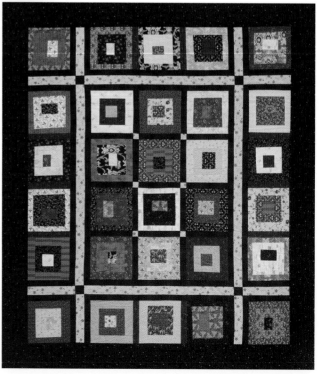

Square in a Square Done Bright

I used 30 blocks to make this little quilt which will be perfect for the next baby that comes along. As I layered my squares I just thought about the contrast between each layer. In some cases there is a higher value contrast than others. I think it's that difference that adds to the whimsical, playful quality of the quilt. I used a very random MFS as I made the blocks.

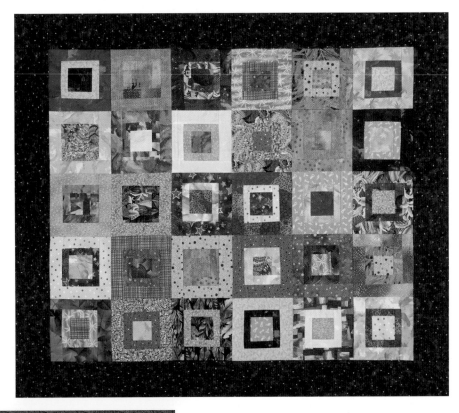

Plaid Squares

I used a lot of flannel plaids, checks, and stripes to make the blocks for this quilt. While I played with a lot more blocks during the design stage, I ended up with 35 blocks set 5 x 7. Doesn't this quilt just make you want to snuggle up in front of the fireplace with a good book and hot cup of tea?

AROUND THE BOX BLOCK

This block is a very old, time-honored pattern, with origins most likely from the basic Log Cabin block. With this new piecing system, I felt it needed a new name. Each Around the Box block has a middle square or rectangle with two rounds of strips framing it.

STARTING SQUARE	MEASUREMENT FOR SLICING*	SQUARING UP SIZE	FINISHED BLOCK SIZE
11"	2", 2", 2", 2" 1 ½", 1 ½", 1 ½", 1 ½"	8 ½"	8"
10"	2", 2", 2", 2" 1 ¼", 1 ¼", 1 ¼", 1 ¼"	7 ½"	7"
9"	1 ½", 1 ½", 1 ½", 1 ½" 1 ¼", 1 ¼", 1 ¼", 1 ¼"	6 ½"	6"

The MFS is meant as a guideline only. I prefer more random numbers, meaning every group of layered fabrics I work with will have a different set of numbers.

NOTE

There is a difference of 3" from the starting square to the finished block size. If you want a different finished block size than I've provided, all you have to do is add 3" to your desired finished size to find the new starting square.

*TIP

Check the first and last fabric squares and make sure the fabrics work well together as they will become part of the same block through the scrambling sequence.

Use the chart at the top of this page to select the finished block size you want to make. Then, use the charts on pages 30-31 to select the size quilt you want to make and see how many blocks you need to make for the size quilt you selected. Remember, if you want a quilt with 24 blocks, you'll begin with 24 squares of fabric, 48 blocks is 48 squares, etc. You're going to lose 2 ½" – 3" between the size squares you start with and the size of your finished blocks. For that reason I've not included 5" starting squares for this particular pattern. I'm sure there are some of you quite capable of working that small with this pattern. If you are, you probably don't need my number help to do it!

LAYER YOUR SQUARES

Select four, six, or eight starting squares of fabric. The fabrics can be high, medium, or low contrast. You can create the contrast through color only, or a combination of color and value. You just want to make sure you can see the difference between the various layers. You also want to make sure you like how the top fabric and the bottom fabric look next to each other.*

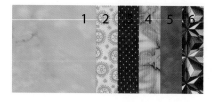

Stack all squares together, RIGHT SIDES UP, aligning the outer edges carefully.

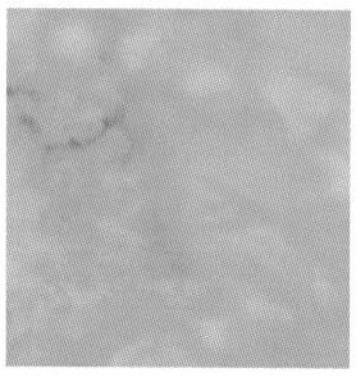

(Six layers in this stack.)

NOTE: I suggest that you make these blocks with an EVEN number of fabrics in the stacks (4, 6, or 8). The more fabrics in your stack, the greater variety you get in your blocks.

SLICE

Using the next four illustrations below as a guide, slice through the stack of squares. You can use the MFS found in the chart at the beginning of this section for a controlled look, or you can change things up with random numbers to achieve an uneven look, as you'll see in the inspiration quilts in this section.

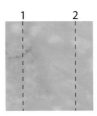

Rotate your mat as needed to make all subsequent cuts.

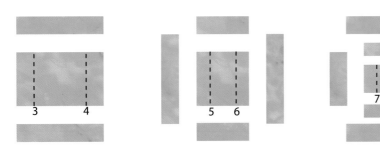

SCRAMBLE

Follow the numbers on the scramble illustration indicating how many pieces to take from the top of each pile and move to the bottom of that same pile. Remember a zero (0) means you leave the pile alone.

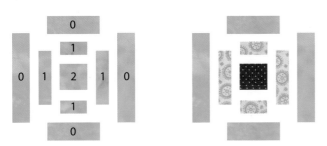

TIP

After each set of slices, move those stacks of pieces away slightly from the rest of the square to prevent cutting into them with subsequent cuts.

TIP

Before you start to scramble, be sure your pieces are positioned as shown in the scramble illustration. This may mean you have to rotate your mat again after making the final slice.

TIP

The pieces that you're adding in any one round should all be the same fabric. If you notice that fabrics aren't the same, you've gotten them out of order. Refer to the Basic Instructions on pages 8 – 9 if you need a refresher on the basic piecing system.

NOTE

Depending on which piece is on top when you sew, your extensions may be at the opposite end than what we show in the illustration. Both give you the same block in the end. You are still going to be trimming all extensions and squaring up all blocks.

SEW

Follow the numbered illustration below for sewing each round.

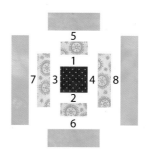

Take the first two pieces of round 1 (seam #1) of the top block and sew them together. Continue with the same seam #1 pieces for block two, block three, etc., all the way to the last block unit.

As described in the Basic Instructions on page 9, clip these like units apart and stack one on top of another ending with the first unit sewn on top. This keeps the units in order.

Finger press the top unit, with seam allowances (S.A.) going away from the center square, and add the next piece (seam #2). Continue sewing with seam #2, one block unit after another. You will finger press one block unit at a time before adding the next seam #2 piece. When they're all sewn, clip and stack as you did above.

Sew seam #3, then seam #4, following the same finger pressing, sewing, clipping, and stacking sequence as you did above. When you are adding these strips (seams #3 and #4), you'll trim the strip extensions after they're sewn, as illustrated. Perfection is not important at this point as you're just trimming excess fabric, you'll square up later.

Continue by adding the next round of strips (seams #5, #6, #7, and #8) in the same way you sewed the last round (seams #1, #2, #3, and #4). Follow the numbered illustration below for the order to sew. Again it will be the top and bottom first, then the two sides. Remember to trim excess strips on the top and bottom pieces before adding the side strips.

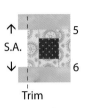 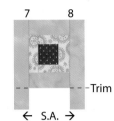

IRON

Once you've sewn all eight seams for your blocks, you can iron. Iron from the wrong side first to make sure all the seam allowances are going away from the inside square. Once you've ironed lightly on the wrong side, turn the block right side up and do a firm ironing.

SQUARE UP

The square up size for your block will vary depending on the size of the fabric square you started with. Refer to the chart on page 18 for this information. If you can't make your blocks the recommended size, don't worry, just make sure all your blocks are the same size, whatever it is.

See page 11 for Finishing Instructions to complete your quilt top.

Field of Boxes — Quilts to Inspire...

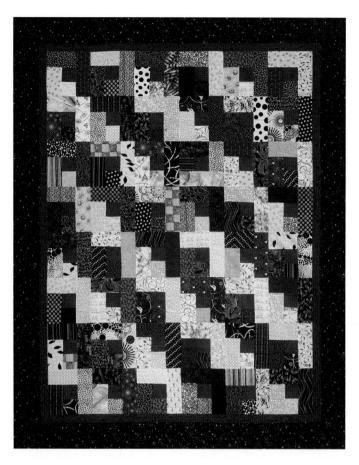

Pat's Black, White, and Red all Over
by Pat Hook

Pat used 24 different white with black squares and 24 different black with white squares to create this bold, graphic quilt. The red centers are just what was needed to punch up the black and white prints. Or was it? What if she'd used yellow, or lime green, or an electric blue? Any of them would have worked and been equally as exciting. Maybe you'd like to make this quilt for a grandson heading to college. Think about the school colors as you select your fabrics.

Controlled

I started this quilt by selecting four companion prints from a single line of fabric. Two similar black prints, and two similar green prints. Next, I picked that rose pink color for the center accent. You do not always have to make your quilts scrappy. I probably prefer scrappy, but sometimes, when you want something quick and easy, then limiting the number of fabrics you use can be the perfect solution.

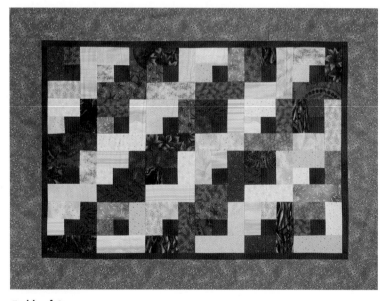

Fields of Green

Well, there's that blue and purple in the field as well, but the green is obviously the dominating color. Even the bright magenta color I selected for the center accent kind of faded away next to the bright greens. I used 24 blocks in this quilt, set 4 x 6.

FIELD OF BOXES BLOCK

STARTING SQUARE	MEASUREMENT FOR SLICING	CENTER REPLACEMENT SQUARES	SQUARING UP SIZE	FINISHED BLOCK SIZE
10"	3 ½"	3"	8 ½"	8"
9"	3"	3"	7 ½"	7"
8"	2 ¾"	2 ½"	6 ½"	6"
5"	1 ¾"	1 ½"	3 ½"	3"

Use the chart above to select the finished block size you want to make. Then, use the charts on pages 30-31 to select the size quilt you want to make and see how many blocks you need to make for the size quilt you selected. Remember, if you want a quilt with 24 blocks, you'll begin with 24 squares of fabric, 48 blocks is 48 squares, etc. In this case, half of those squares will be one color and half will be another color.

In this block, we will replace the center square with one accent fabric. To cut your center replacement squares, use the calculations in the chart below.

STRIP SIZE	SQUARE YIELD
3" x width of fabric	13 squares per strip
2 ½" x width of fabric	16 squares per strip
1 ½" x width of fabric	26 squares per strip

NOTE

There is a difference of 2" from the starting square to the finished block size. If you want a different finished block size than I've provided, all you have to do is add 2" to your desired finished size to find the new starting square.

Select three different colors for this pattern. One of the colors being the accent square in the center of the block. The other two colors will frame that center square, one color on one side, the other color on the other side.

We'll use Pat's black, white, and red quilt as our example. For the 48 blocks in her quilt she needed 24 different white fabric squares and 24 different black fabric squares. She started with 10" squares. Her red squares were 3" cut size. She needed a total of 48, 3" red squares. One strip of fabric cut at 3" will yield 13 squares. This means she needed four 3" strips of red, sub-cut into 3" squares.

LAYER YOUR SQUARES

Select four starting squares of fabric, two of your first fabric color, and two of the second fabric color. Remember, each square is a different fabric. Layer the fabrics Color 1 (Black), Color 2 (White), Color 3 (Black), Color 4 (White). Black and white are for our example only. You can use your own color combination.

Stack all squares together, RIGHT SIDES UP, aligning the outer edges carefully.

(Four layers in this stack.)

SLICE

Using the illustration below as a guide, slice through the stack of squares. The chart at the beginning of this section gave you some possible measurements to use. Feel free to change them as desired.

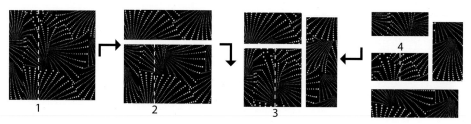

After the first cut you will rotate the mat one quarter turn to the right (clockwise) and make the second cut. After each cut you will move that section of pieces away, turn the mat a quarter turn to the right, slice, etc.

TIP

After each slice make sure that you move that stack of pieces slightly away from the rest of the pieces to prevent cutting into them with the subsequent cut.

TIP

Before you start to scramble, be sure your pieces are positioned as shown in the scramble illustration. This may mean you have to rotate your mat again after making the final slice.

SCRAMBLE

Follow the numbered illustration below to know how many pieces to move from the top of that stack to the bottom. Remember, the center square is going to be replaced, so once cut, simply remove the original square stack and replace it with your accent color squares.

SEW

Follow the numbers for sewing.

Take the first two pieces of the top block and sew them together. Continue with the first two pieces of block two, then block three, etc., all the way to the last block unit. As described on page 9 of the Basic Instructions, clip the units apart and stack one on top of another.

Finger press the top unit with the seam allowance (S.A.) going away from the center square. Continue sewing with seam #2, one block after another. Repeat with seam #3 and then #4, always finger pressing the S.A. away from the center square before adding the next piece.

IRON

Now you can go to the ironing board and iron the blocks. Iron from the wrong side first to make sure the seam allowances are doing what they are supposed to be doing, which is always going away from that inside square. Once you've lightly ironed from the wrong side, turn the block over, right side up, and do a firm ironing.

SQUARE UP

The square up size for your block will vary depending on the size of the fabric square you started with. Refer to the chart on page 23 for this information. If you can't make your blocks the recommended size, don't worry, just make sure all your blocks are the same size, whatever it is.

LAY OUT YOUR BLOCKS AS DESIRED

To create the Fields and Furrows design, alternate the block with two long blacks with a block with two long whites. Think of the long sides as creating an "L" shape.

This is where a flannel wall is very helpful. You can place all the blocks on the flannel wall before starting to sew them together. It doesn't make any difference how many blocks you have across and down, the layout will remain the same, alternating the long side colors.

"What IF?" . . . What if you didn't lay your blocks out this way? Feel free to play with your blocks to come up with a different arrangement that you like. You might even want to put sashing between the blocks. The possibilities are endless!

See page 11 for Finishing Instructions to complete your quilt top.

Condo Box — Quilts to Inspire...

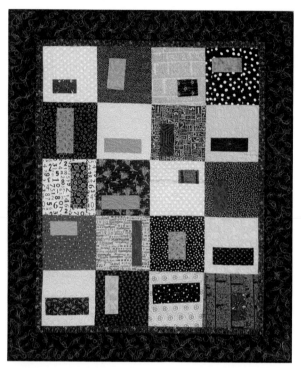

Confetti Towers

In this quilt, I chose to use only one light fabric and lots of different brights. There are 35 blocks in the quilt, which means I started with 18 white squares and 18 bright squares. Yes, I had one leftover block when I was done. But someday that block will appear in one of my other quilts. We have to work with even numbers when making the blocks, but our quilts don't always end up using an even number of blocks.

Condo Contemporary

I liked the colors so much in the Band Box 3 quilt (page 12) that I knew I wanted to make a Condo quilt with similar fabrics. I will tell you, however, in creating these blocks, I worked more like the Field of Boxes design, in that I substituted the window fabric, rather than scrambling to achieve the accent. I knew I didn't want red or blue in the outside positions of the blocks, but I did want them in the inner window area. So rather than making a bunch of blocks I wouldn't use, I just cut a replacement piece for the window section using the accent colors I wanted. You can still layer and cut the same way, just remove and replace, rather than scramble. I also used more random MFS here for slicing, rather than the consistent ones as seen in the other two quilts on this page.

Condo On Point

I used very controlled measurements when cutting these 18 blocks, but made it more whimsical by the random placement of that "window" position. I used one consistent fabric for the side and corner triangles. Check the chart on page 31 for triangle specifics.

CONDO BOX BLOCK

STARTING SQUARE	MEASUREMENT FOR SLICING*	SQUARING UP SIZE	FINISHED BLOCK SIZE
10"	2 ½", 2½"	8 ½"	8"
	2 ½", 4"		
9"	2 ½", 2 ½"	7 ½"	7"
	2 ¼", 4"		
8"	2", 2"	6 ½"	6"
	2", 3 ½"		
5"	1 ½", 1 ½"	3 ½"	3"
	1 ¼", 2"		

*The top line of numbers represents the vertical cuts, the bottom set of numbers is for slicing the center section.

Using the chart at the top of this page, pick the finished block size you want to make. Then, using the charts on pages 30-31, select the size quilt you want to make and see how many blocks you need to make for the size quilt you selected. Remember, if you want a quilt with 24 blocks, you'll begin with 24 squares of fabric, 48 blocks is 48 squares, etc.

LAYER YOUR SQUARES

Select six starting squares of fabric. I recommend a higher contrast between the layers in this pattern. Again, make sure you like the way the first and last fabrics look next to one another as they will make a block together. Each block is made of only two fabrics. You could work with only two layers at a time if you so desired. If you do this, then the fabrics would simply alternate position. The more fabrics you layer, the more variety you'll have in your blocks.

For our example here, we're using a selection of fabrics similar to Confetti Towers (page 26) with one light fabric alternating with a variety of bright fabrics.

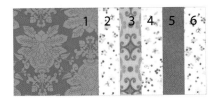

Stack all squares together, RIGHT SIDES UP, aligning the outer edges carefully.

(Six layers in this stack.)

When I first started working on layouts with this block, they reminded me of a high rise apartment or condominium complex. The little pieces in the center of the block became their doors — or windows! The name just stuck, and I can't look at one of these quilts without wondering what's going on inside that little unit.

NOTE

There is a difference of 2" from the starting square to the finished block size. If you want a different finished block size than I've provided, all you have to do is add 2" to your desired finished size to find the new starting square.

SLICE

Refer to the chart on page 27 to determine the Measurement for Slicing (MFS). Remember, this is a guideline. You may change the numbers however you'd like. Be sure and notice that there are two sets of numbers this time.

Vertical slices first as illustrated.

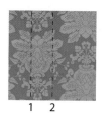

1   2

Move the two outside segments aside. Turn the mat a quarter turn to the left and slice the middle section according to the MFS (or whatever measurements you select). Two of the inspiration quilts were very controlled in these slicing numbers, the third quilt was totally random. Think about your options.

3   4

SCRAMBLE

Only one piece gets scrambled in this block. Follow the illustration below and move one piece as shown. Remember, you may need to rotate your mat after making your final slice and before scrambling, so that your pieces match the illustration.

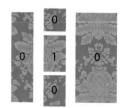

SEW

Sew the middle section first, then add on the two outside edges. All seam allowances (S.A.) go away from the center "window" or "door."

↑
S.A.   1
↓   2

3   4

←S.A.→

IRON

Iron wrong side up first to make sure the seam allowances are doing what they should. Turn the block over right side up and do a firm ironing.

SQUARE UP

The square up size for your block will vary depending on the size of the fabric square you started with. Refer to the chart on page 27 for this information. If you can't make your blocks the recommended size, don't worry, just make sure all your blocks are the same size, whatever it is. Like some of the other blocks, you can square up off-kilter if you choose to.

See page 11 for Finishing Instructions to complete the quilt top.

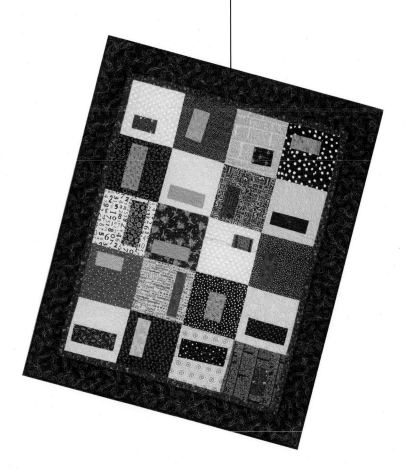

STRAIGHT SET

NOTE

Finished top without borders shown in **blue**.

Finished top with recommended borders shown in **red**.

BORDERS

3" Blocks

- Cut 1" for the first border (Accent Border).
- Cut 2 ½" for the second border (Framing Border).

6", 7", and 8" Blocks

- Cut 1 ½" for first border (Accent Border).
- Cut 5 ½" for second border (Framing Border).

SET	TOTAL # OF BLOCKS*	FINISHED BLOCK SIZE			
		3"	6"	7"	8"
3 x 4	12	9" x 12"	18" x 24"	21" x 28"	24" x 32"
		14" x 17"	30" x 36"	33" x 40"	36" x 44"
4 x 5	20	12" x 15"	24" x 30"	28" x 35"	32" x 40"
		17" x 20"	36" x 42"	40" x 47"	44" x 52"
4 x 6	24	12" x 18"	24" x 36"	28" x 42"	32" x 48"
		17" x 23"	36" x 48"	40" x 54"	44" x 60"
5 x 7	35	15" x 21"	30" x 42"	35" x 49"	40" x 56"
		20" x 26"	42" x 54"	47" x 61"	52" x 68"
6 x 7	42	18" x 21"	36" x 42"	42" x 49"	48" x 56"
		23" x 26"	48" x 54"	54" x 61"	60" x 68"
6 x 8	48	18" x 24"	36" x 48"	42" x 56"	48" x 64"
		23" x 29"	48" x 60"	54" x 68"	60" x 76"
8 x 10	80	24" x 30"	48" x 60"	56" x 70"	64" x 80"
		29" x 35"	60" x 72"	68" x 82"	76" x 92"
9 x 12	108	27" x 36"	54" x 72"	63" x 84"	72" x 96"
		32" x 41"	66" x 84"	75" x 96"	84" x 108"
10 x 12	120	30" x 36"	60" x 72"	70" x 84"	80" x 96"
		35" x 41"	72" x 84"	82" x 96"	92" x 108"
12 x 14	168	36" x 42"	72" x 84"	84" x 98"	96" x 112"
		41" x 47"	84" x 96"	96" x 110"	108" x 124"

*Total number of blocks represents both the number of squares to begin with, AND the number of finished blocks.

Straight Set 3 x 4

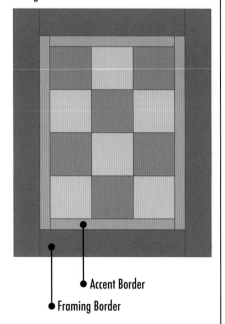

Accent Border

Framing Border

Type	Mattress Size	Basic Size (Including Borders)
Nap	n/a	48" x 60"
Crib	23" x 46"	36" x 48"
Twin	39" x 75"	60" x 96"
Full	54" x 75"	78" x 96"
Queen	60" x 80"	84" x 102"
King	72" x 84"	96" x 108"

DIAGONAL SET

| SET | TOTAL # OF BLOCKS* | FINISHED BLOCK SIZE | | | | # of Side Set Triangles Needed |
		3"	6"	7"	8"	
2 x 3	8	8 ½" x 12 ¾"	17" x 25 ½"	19 ¾" x 29 ¾"	22 ½" x 34"	6
		13 ½" x 17 ¾"	29" x 37 ½"	31 ¾" x 41 ¾"	34 ½" x 46"	
3 x 4	18	12 ¾" x 17"	25 ½" x 34"	29 ¾" x 39 ½"	34" x 45 ¼"	10
		17 ¾" x 22"	37 ½" x 46"	41 ¾" x 51 ½"	46" x 57 ½"	
4 x 5	32	17" x 21 ¼"	34" x 42 ½"	39 ½" x 49 ½"	45 ¼" x 56 ½"	14
		22" x 26 ¼"	46" x 54 ½"	51 ½" x 61 ½"	57 ¼" x 68 ½"	
4 x 6	39	17" x 25 ½"	34" x 51"	39 ½" x 59 ¼"	45 ¼" x 68"	16
		22" x 30 ½"	46" x 63"	51 ½" x 71 ¼"	57 ½" x 80"	
5 x 7	59	21 ¼" x 29 ¾"	42 ½" x 59 ½"	49 ½" x 69 ¼"	56 ½" x 79 ¼"	20
		26 ¼" x 34 ¾"	54 ½" x 71 ½"	61 ½" x 81 ¼"	68 ½" x 91"	
6 x 8	83	25 ½" x 34"	51" x 68"	59 ¼" x 79"	68" x 90 ½"	24
		30 ½" x 39"	63" x 80"	71 ¼" x 91"	80" x 102 ½"	
8 x 10	143	34" x 42 ½"	68" x 84 ¾"	79" x 98"	90 ½" x 113"	32
		39" x 47 ½"	80" x 96 ¾"	91" x 110"	102 ½" x 125"	

*Total number of blocks represents both the number of squares to begin with, AND the number of finished blocks.

SETTING TRIANGLES		
Block Size	Side	Corner
3"	5 ½" ⊠	3" ◺
6"	9 ¾" ⊠	5 ⅛" ◺
7"	11 ¼" ⊠	5 ⅞" ◺
8"	12 ⅝" ⊠	6 ⅝" ◺

NOTE

Finished top without borders shown in blue.

Finished top with borders shown in red.

BORDERS

3" Blocks
- Cut 1" for the first border (Accent Border).
- Cut 2 ½" for the second border (Framing Border).

6", 7", and 8" Blocks
- Cut 1 ½" for first border (Accent Border).
- Cut 5 ½" for second border (Framing Border).

Diagonal Set 2 x 3

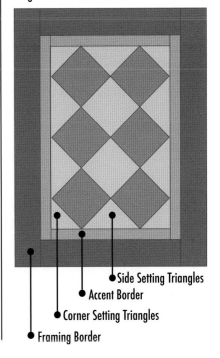

Side Setting Triangles
Accent Border
Corner Setting Triangles
Framing Border

About the Author

Sharyn Craig

In 1978, when Sharyn took her first quilting class, she had no idea what direction her life was going to take. She was immediately obsessed with making quilts. Soon she was figuring out ways to make quilts using easier, more organized, and more efficient methods. Next came the opportunity to share those skills with others. She taught quilting through adult education classes and the local quilt shops first. As early as 1983 she was leaving the security of her home territory to share those skills with more quilters. When she retired in 2009, she'd taught in 47 states in the United States and five foreign countries. In 1985, she was named the outstanding Quilt Teacher of the Year by the Professional Quilter magazine.

Sharyn has written numerous magazine articles and books. Her book titles include *The Art of Classic Quiltmaking* (co-authored with Harriet Hargrave), *Designing New Traditions in Quilts, Drafting Plus, Setting Solutions, Great Sets, Twist 'n Turn, Half Log Cabin Quilts, Layer 'em Up Volume 1: Xs and More,* and *Quilt Challenge: "What If" Ideas for Color and Design* (co-authored with Pamela Mostek).

Sharyn lives in the San Diego, California area with her husband, George. She is the mother of two married children and grandmother to three wonderful grandchildren.

"In my soul I will always be a teacher.
I will always share my love and passion for quilting."
Sharyn Squier Craig

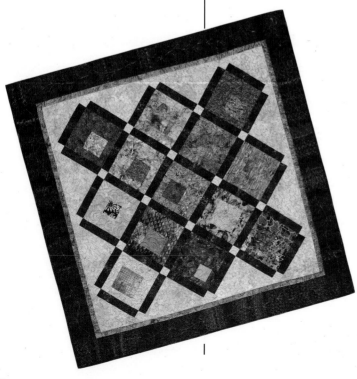